Garden of the Gods

Photographs by
Todd Caudle

Skyline Press
Pueblo, Colorado

Garden of the Gods

Photographs by
Todd Caudle

Published by Skyline Press
311 West Evans Avenue
Pueblo, Colorado 81004
ISBN: 1-888845-05-8
Printed in Hong Kong

Front Cover: Morning light on Kissing Camels
Back Cover: Garden panorama
Facing Page: Sunflowers below Kissing Camels

Colorado Souvenir Series

Introduction

When I published my first book on the Pikes Peak region, I wondered quietly if it would be a kind of artistic exorcism. That is, I wondered whether or not I would still feel compelled to spend so many early mornings and late evenings watching the sun paint Garden of the Gods and Pikes Peak with its magnificence. After all, for years I had spent so much time lugging camera gear along the trails of the Garden of the Gods, and I had witnessed Pikes Peak awash in the light of so many incredible sunrises — would I still have something artistic to say?

It didn't take long to answer my own question. No sooner was the first book off to the printer than I found myself greeting sunrise beneath the ages-old rocks of Garden of the Gods. For three consecutive days after shipping the book, there I was, camera and tripod in tow, looking for great light and new angles to photograph. It was clear that these lofty subjects still had a firm grip on my soul.

In compiling the images for this book, I tried to avoid simply rehashing the Garden of the Gods portfolio from my previous book, "Pikes Peak and Garden of the Gods — Two Worlds, One Vision." Because the landscape of Garden of the Gods is so rich with diversity, that wasn't a difficult task. Yet, time and time again I was drawn back to places I had visited and photographed before, and saw them in a whole new light. Perhaps an unusual cloud, a different season, shadows cast in a way I hadn't seen before — many of the places I had photographed before presented themselves differently to me the next time around. As a result, this book is an amalgam of old and new, of changing seasons and circumstance.

Do I still feel an insatiable need to keep photographing Garden of the Gods and Pikes Peak? You bet! I've found that, like a painter who paints a self-portrait to keep his technique sharp, visiting these places again and again enhances my vision as I travel around Colorado and the West, chasing those ever-elusive moments when everything beautiful — light, subject and circumstance — falls into place within the context of my camera's viewfinder.

—Todd Caudle

Left: Breaking storm and alpenglow light

Spring
a new beginning

Hale-Bopp Comet, 1997

Tower of Babel and sandstone frame

Piñon pine silhouette at sunrise
Left: Stormy light, late spring

Balanced Rock

Moonset and the Siamese Twins

Yuccas with seed pods
Left: Kissing Camels and one-seed juniper frame

Springtime meadow and Cathedral Rock
Right: Cottonwood trees and South Gateway Rock

Cottonwood detail

Cathedral Rock reflection

Summer

season of the sun

Left: Summer sunflowers
Overleaf: Pikes Peak and Garden of the Gods

Moonset framed in Kissing Camels

Moonrise and ancient junipers

Yuccas below Kissing Camels

Juniper below the Three Graces

Summer silhouettes — Kissing Camels (above) and the Three Graces (left)

Sunflowers and morning light

Golden banner wildflowers

Pine cones

Morning light and the Gateway
Left: Moonset over Kissing Camels

Autumn
of changing colors

Left: Autumn colors in the central Garden area

Sandstone monoliths

Tower of Babel
Overleaf: Autumn palette

Crescent moon over the Three Graces

Kissing Camels and full moon

Barren oak

Bare cottonwood and Pikes Peak

Autumn gold below Cathedral Rock
Right: White Rock and Kissing Camels in pastel light

Autumn brilliance

Yucca and changing oak leaves

Cathedral Rock
Left: Balanced Rock

Winter

the land sleeps

Left: One-seed juniper frame and South Gateway Rock

Fresh snow
Left: Clearing storm

Fresh snow on the Giant Footprints
Preceding pages: Winter panorama

Cathedral Rock and Spire and the Three Graces

Cathedral Spire and the Three Graces
Right: Fresh snow on Kissing Camels

Rime ice below Kissing Camels

Balanced Rock in winter

About the Photographer

Todd Caudle has been photographing the natural world for nearly twenty years. His work has appeared in a variety of regional and national publications, including Shutterbug, Rolling Stone, the Rocky Mountain News and the Colorado Springs Gazette. His photographs have been selected for the covers of the Colorado Official State Vacation Guide and the Colorado Springs Visitors Guide, and his work has been exhibited at the Colorado Springs Fine Arts Center and the Pikes Peak Library Gallery. The photographer of three previous books, including "Pikes Peak and Garden of the Gods — Two Worlds, One Vision," and numerous scenic calendars, Todd lives in Pueblo with his wife, Barbara, and their dogs, Sierra and Cheyenne.

TO KNOW A STARRY NIGHT

White Rim Trail, Canyonlands National Park, Utah

to know a starry night

PAUL BOGARD

WITH PHOTOGRAPHY BY
BEAU ROGERS

UNIVERSITY OF NEVADA PRESS | *Reno & Las Vegas*

University of Nevada Press | Reno, Nevada 89557 USA
www.unpress.nevada.edu
Copyright © 2021 by Paul Bogard
All rights reserved
Photographs © 2021 by Beau Rogers
Book and jacket design by Jinni Fontana

LIBRARY OF CONGRESS CATALOGING-IN-PUBLICATION DATA
Names: Bogard, Paul, 1966- author. | Rogers, Beau, 1974- photographer.
Title: To know a starry night : an exploration of the experience / by Paul Bogard;
    photography by Beau Rogers.
Description: Reno ; Las Vegas : University of Nevada Press, [2021] |
Summary: "This book explores the experience of being outside under a natural
    starry sky—how important it is to human life, and how so many people don't
    know this experience. It combines the lyrical writing of Paul Bogard with the
    night-sky photography of Beau Rogers. There are nine chapters."—Provided
    by publisher
Identifiers: LCCN 2021008768 | ISBN 9781647790127 (cloth) | ISBN 9781647790134
    (ebook)
Subjects: LCSH: Bogard, Paul, 1966- | Light pollution. | Night—Psychological
    aspects. | Lighting—Psychological aspects. | Lighting—Social aspects. |
    Sky—Pictorial works. | Night photography.
Classification: LCC TD195.L52 B65 2021 | DDC 551.56/6—dc23
LC record available at https://lccn.loc.gov/2021008768

The paper used in this book meets the requirements of American National
Standard for Information Sciences—Permanence of Paper for Printed Library
Materials, ANSI/NISO Z39.48-1992 (R2002).

FIRST PRINTING

Printed in Canada

Grand Tetons National Park, Wyoming

CONTENTS

Second Beach, Olympic National Park, Washington

Night—like air, like water, is one of the great equalizers in nature. It is available somehow to all of us, no matter where we live on the planet, no matter what language we speak or what culture shapes our world-view. We experience night with such routineness that—as with daytime—we take it for granted; it recedes into the background of our lives. Thus, "to know a starry night," to really know and attend to the beauty and meaning of a dark and starry night, is an exceedingly rare experience. Such an experience is available to most of us in the world day after day, and yet it takes a trigger of some kind to guide us to notice and dwell on the exquisite gift of a dark and star-filled sky.

Paul Bogard opens his introduction to this book with a strange quotation from Ralph Waldo Emerson's classic essay "Nature": "If the stars should appear one night in a thousand years…" The epigraph trails off into Bogard's own reverie about sharing the night sky with his infant daughter, which is, in fact, how I believe we should always read literature and art, as windows to the world and to our own lives. But in the original text, Emerson continues his thinking about the stars by writing, "how would men believe and adore; and preserve for many generations the remembrance of the city of God which had been shown! But every night come out these envoys of beauty, and light the universe with their admonishing smile" (5). This admonishing smile may be nature's way of saying, "Wake up! Pay attention! You are missing something at once commonplace and extraordinary!" In fact, a few lines later in the essay,

Emerson quips in a strangely understated way, "Nature never wears a mean appearance." This last line, often quoted by scholars and enthusiasts of transcendentalism, has often puzzled me. It is a quiet way of saying that nature is always beautiful and worthy of our reverence and attention.

No matter where we are or who we are, no matter our status in society, we almost always have some access to the sky. Emerson suggests that the stars inspire reverence "because though always present, they are inaccessible." I beg to differ. Of course we cannot directly touch the stars as we might place our hand on a tree or shuffle through the foamy surf as it spreads across a beach, but unless we're visually impaired, we do have access to the sky through our eyes. And we do have access through our imaginations.

Ken Lamberton, who has an entire book (*Wilderness and Razor Wire*) about experiencing the beauties of nature while in prison, writes in an essay titled "How Nature Taught Me to Sing in Lockup" that access to wild beauty "lessen[s] the darkness" of a brutal place, such as the heavy gray walls of a prison. Though not free to wander outside and stargaze, during his years of incarceration Lamberton was able to glimpse the landscape through a narrow window near his upper bunk, where, "On some evenings, coyotes called to me with borderless voices from the desert's fringe where nighthawks knit the sky with needled wings." He doesn't mention stars here per se, but he suggests that the sounds of night and visual emblems other than stars reached him even in his cell.

We might also expect visual access to the starry sky to be relatively limited in a city flooded with artificial light. But Toni Morrison writes lyrically of the power of the night sky as glimpsed and imagined by her urban characters in the novel *Jazz*. She laments the fact that many in the city "when they do not forget the sky completely think of it as a tiny piece of information about the time of day or night." In reality, says her narrator, "there is nothing to beat what the City can make of a nightsky. It can empty itself of surface, and more like the ocean than the ocean itself, go deep, starless,...booming over a glittering city" (35). When we can't see the sky itself, we can sometimes glimpse the darting wings of nighthawks, and when the city glare overcomes distant starlight, the blare and crash of an urban soundscape become an astral symphony.

Although people throughout the world, in one way or another, have access to the beauty and mystery that is the night sky and to the full range of human emotions inspired by the experience of night, there may be something particularly potent about the experience of night in the American West, as in other arid regions where the sky looms large and maintains a strong sensory presence in our lives. I was raised in Oregon's gray and foggy Willamette Valley, where I'd often go weeks at a time without being able to see the stars at night. Perhaps, with regard to stargazing, a boyhood under cloudy skies is a little bit like being in prison or like living in a glittery city where "thrilling, wasteful street lamps" (34), to use Morrison's words again, occlude the brilliant reality above that we know is there even though we can't physically perceive it. When we're prevented from experiencing the brilliance of the night sky and then are suddenly exposed to the stars, we feel a sense of overwhelming gratitude, or at least this is what I feel. I want to gaze myself into space—to launch myself through my eyes—so I never forget the experience and can summon it no matter how limited my actual view.

As a teenager, I sought every opportunity to backpack in the Three Sisters Wilderness east of Eugene, camping out under the stars with high school friends,

Second Beach, Olympic National Park, Washington

stars we could seldom see through the coastal atmosphere at home in Eugene. Since those days, I have experienced night skies in many parts of the world, urban and wild, Nordic and tropical, temperate and arid. I spent a year in the mid-nineties living in the dazzlingly overlit alleyways of the Ikebukuro district, Tokyo, Japan, where the night sky was a distant memory. My nature writing colleagues and I had no hope of glimpsing starlight while running five-kilometer loops around the Imperial Palace or when crisscrossing the city in subterranean trains. But even in Japan, when I traveled to Hokkaido or Aomori for hiking and lecture trips, vast starscapes came into view at night. In recent years, I've had the good fortune of teaching occasionally at one of the most remote academic outposts in North America, the University of Idaho's Taylor Wilderness Research Station, located in the heart of the Frank Church–River of No Return Wilderness, where the midnight sky is a sea of light, utterly unblemished by technological constellations of headlights and illuminated buildings down on Earth.

Everywhere I travel—Toulouse or Istanbul, Cape Town or Beijing, Uluru or Guam—I find myself gazing upward, searching for something, probably for glimpses of skyward wonder I remember fleetingly from my boyhood in the cloudy part of Oregon. As an occasional insomniac and a lover of the outdoors, I often find myself outside at odd hours. In Finland, jet-lagged, I routinely go for a run on lamplit, snow-slicked streets in winter or oddly sunlit forest paths at two o'clock in the morning in May, when stars would be visible if I were in the outback of the western United States. . . or in Australia. At home in Idaho in recent years, and now at my new home in Oregon again, when awake at an odd hour, I go outside with my dog, sit on the grass, and gaze up, listening to night sounds, taking in the darkness, and squinting to see bits of the Milky Way.

In recent months, while experiencing unprecedented wildfires in the

American West, I've found myself thinking a lot about not only urban light pollution and naturally cloudy skies, but about the AQI (air quality index), which indicates both the level of harmful particulates in the air and visibility. Through either excessive light or unintended particulates in the atmosphere, we are causing what Robert Michael Pyle has called "the extinction of experience" (*Thunder Tree* 146). He meant that city kids are now spending less and less time in the woods and fields, in nearby wild places; but our twenty-first-century exposure to unobstructed night skies, in urban and suburban settings and even in rural and wild locations during times of smoke-choked air, has also become increasingly precious as we suffer the extinction of this form of experience.

"If the stars should appear one night in a thousand years," writes Emerson. Although the stars and the beauty of deep, dark space are in no danger of disappearing, the reality of our twenty-first-century lives is that most people do not see or think about the starry sky, do not really *know* it. This is where wonderful writers and visual artists like Paul Bogard and Beau Rogers come in.

I have known Paul and Beau for many years, since our time together at the University of Nevada, Reno, where I taught from 1996 to 2012 in the English Department's Literature and Environment Program and where Paul was a doctoral student and Beau earned his master's degree. While working on other projects for his PhD, Paul also published the anthology *Let There Be Night: Testimony on Behalf of the Dark* and laid the groundwork for his first book of nonfiction, *The End of Night: Searching for Darkness in an Age of Artificial Light*. Beau, meanwhile, began spending much of his spare time roaming the remote corners of the Great Basin Desert and the Sierra Nevadas with his cameras, composing extraordinary photos, including many night shots, of western American landscapes.

As the years passed, it occurred to me that Paul and Beau would make an amazing team if they considered working together on a project to bring together words and images in a call for less light pollution, less air pollution, and more attention to the value of nighttime darkness. So I planted a seed with my two friends. This exquisite book, *To Know a Starry Night,* is the result of their collaboration. The three of us hope this work will bring pleasure to those who read it, of course, but we also hope it will inspire readers to look up from the pages and think about the meaning of dark skies in their own lives.

"Nature never wears a mean appearance," says Emerson. And this is true no matter where we are. But we sometimes need reminders, prompts to pay attention and really think about what we take for granted. That's the work of books like this one.

—Scott Slovic, Eugene, Oregon

REFERENCES

Bogard, Paul. *The End of Night: Searching for Darkness in an Age of Artificial Light.* Little, Brown, 2013.
———. *Let There Be Night: Testimony on Behalf of the Dark.* Reno: University of Nevada Press, 2008.
Emerson, Ralph Waldo. "Nature" (1836). In *The Complete Essays and Other Writings of Ralph Waldo Emerson,* edited by Brooks Atkinson, 5–42. New York: Modern Library, 1950.
Lamberton, Ken. "How Nature Taught Me to Sing in Lockup." *Rain Shadow Review,* September 2, 2017. https://rainshadowreview .com/first-blog-post/.
———. *Wilderness and Razor Wire: A Naturalist's Observations from Prison.* San Francisco: Mercury House, 2000.
Morrison, Toni. *Jazz.* New York: Penguin, 1992.
Pyle, Robert Michael. *The Thunder Tree: Lessons from an Urban Wildland.* Boston: Houghton Mifflin, 1993.

TO KNOW A STARRY NIGHT

Point Reyes Shipwreck, Inverness, California

introduction

If the stars should appear one night in a thousand years…

—Ralph Waldo Emerson, "Nature"

On my daughter's first night home, two days after her birth, I took her to see the stars. I wrapped her in fleece, held her close, and stepped out into a late spring night. Just above a neighbor's roofline I found the setting moon among a handful of bright stars and lifted her toward the sky—a sight that with its steady distant fires will accompany her, no matter the changes, all through her life. That a newborn human can see only inches from their face, and therefore not really the universe, I didn't yet know. I just knew that I couldn't wait to share this nighttime world with my daughter.

We live in the southern half of a northern city, and while the grounds behind our house are somewhat dark, the sky is clogged with artificial light. Like almost any city anywhere, ours uses light haphazardly, wastefully, sending much of it skyward to disrupt insects, confuse night-migrating birds, and wipe away the stars. So, those stars we saw that first night were far fewer than a father and his child would have seen just decades ago, a remnant from a hundred years past. This chasing away of darkness has happened relatively recently, after night being the same since the beginning of time. Almost anywhere people live in any number shares this truth: we have taken what was one of the most common human experiences—walking out at night and coming face to face with the universe—and made it one of the most rare.

And still. Night is half our life and darkness a natural part of what it means to be alive. Beauty dwells here, and calm. I think of the poet Wendell Berry waking in the night "in fear of what my life and my children's lives may be" and finding among night birds "the peace of wild things." For me, night has always been a time of rest and reflection, of dreams and freedom, of longing and peace. I hope it will be the same for my daughter. I know that especially for women we have too often made it something to fear. But that's on us, not on darkness. There is nothing inherently evil about the dark. Traditional societies and poets have known this forever, and now modern science tells us the same: life on Earth evolved with bright days and dark nights, and we need both for optimal health—for our body, our mind, our spirit.

And there still are places we can experience natural darkness. Places where the Milky Way bends from horizon to horizon, where no artificial lights break the timeless view. I think especially of our national parks and reserves, most created with daytime scenery in mind and not a thought to night. But in an age where we live increasingly immersed in artificial light, these protected places hold some of our best remaining natural darkness. Yes, such darkness still exists over the oceans, over remote lands where few ever go. But in the places where most of us live, we are losing or have lost our view of the stars. These wild protected places can remind us what has been lost or, increasingly, show us what we have never known.

I count myself lucky. The year I was born my parents drove me three hours north to a cabin newly built. Here, all my life, on a northern lake in the forest, I have known natural darkness. I have heard wolves along the horizon, owls

Salton Sea, California

Cathedral Rock, Sedona, Arizona

among the pines, loons across still water. I have lain back on the snow-covered frozen lake with binoculars, pouring countless stars into my eyes. In my oldest memory I am five years old and standing on the dock with my father watching satellites cut straight lines through sugary spreads of stars.

And I have been lucky to travel to stars—from the Serengeti Plain, to the English Channel "dark sky island" of Sark, to a Moroccan Sahara night so plush with starlight that when I woke and walked outside my first thought was snow.

In the American West, I have been fortunate to live close to my country's darkest star-strewn landscapes and national parks—Great Basin, Death Valley, Grand Canyon, and on. This book emerges from the American West in part because both Beau and I have long loved its geography of night. The wide-open vistas, the basins and mountain ranges, the long rivers and deep lakes—here is where so much of our best darkness remains. Here is where so many Americans and people from all over the world come to see a sky they no longer see where they live. That said, the images and words we share in this book are meant to help preserve night's natural beauty wherever it may be found. We use night in the American West to celebrate an experience worth knowing wherever we call home.

Even in a book full of photographs, it's worth remembering that it is not just the sight of stars that makes this experience, but all our senses engaged. The summer's symphony of insects, the drifting scent of autumn's change, the dry desert air against your bare skin, or a sleeping child held firmly against your chest—I want my daughter to have this experience. I want her to know in the numbers and distances the sensation of having her mind overwhelmed. To feel awe and exhilaration, to ask the questions such an experience naturally brings. Wrote Henry Beston in the 1920s of the Cape Cod night, "When the

Delamar Dry Lake, Nevada

great earth, abandoning day, rolls up the deeps of the heavens and the universe, a new door opens for the human spirit, and there are few so clownish that some awareness of the mystery of being does not touch them as they gaze." I want the "mystery of being" to be part of her life, something to visit and take in, something to sit with for a while.

This is a book about the experience of being outside with a naturally dark night sky. It's a book about the qualities that together make an experience that humans have known forever but that now, in our time, is fading from our lives. It's a book about what we have lost and are losing, but also what we can preserve and regain.

"If the stars should appear one night in a thousand years," argued Ralph Waldo Emerson in 1836, "how men would believe and adore; and preserve for many generations the remembrance of the city of God which had been shown!" Even in an age of artificial light, most of us live where we can at least see a handful of stars, and sometimes—in our darkest places—many times more. But if we are to "preserve for many generations" this experience we have known, now is the time to act. For my child and every child, and for all those to come.

Let us bring them to the stars as soon and as often as we can.

Green River Overlook, Canyonlands National Park, Utah

darkness

In a dark time, the eye begins to see

—Theodore Roethke, "In a Dark Time"

On the darkest night I have ever known I said goodbye to a friend and started walking back to my family's cabin. Between those points lay a hundred yards of dark woods, maybe the darkest they had ever been. It was a cloudy night with no moon or stars, and only a few lights around the lake. Seven years old, I walked slowly—eyes adjusting as they could, dry pine needles beneath my steps—until I made it about halfway, then stopped. I could no longer see the light from my neighbor's doorway and could not yet see the light from ours. I couldn't even see my hand before my face. The woods around me were filled with animals beginning to move, to use the cover of darkness to live. In the ground beneath me, in constant dark, were the countless creatures that keep the forest soil alive. Above me, beyond the clouds, were layered blankets of stars. Inside me, amid the dark miracles of blood, muscle, and bone, my heart beat fast. But otherwise, I was alone. In this darkness I felt submerged, the presence pressing from all sides. I looked up past the pines to where, on a clear night, constellations would shine, but tonight a cloudy black wool came down to the treetops. Who knew what else this darkness might hold? When I caught brief sight through the pines of our cabin door's glow, I took off.

I ran down the one-lane road, kicking sandy gravel behind, and didn't stop

Death Valley National Park, California

Downtown Los Angeles, California

until I reached the light. I raced across the front yard—the same yard where for a lifetime I have stood in awe beneath the Milky Way—and didn't pause in leaving the dark behind.

I think of that darkness now, so many years later. Peppered with stars, washed by moonlight, the same natural darkness every night for all of time before that moment. I feel grateful to have known it as a child, to have such darkness a part of me that won't ever leave.

——

I want my daughter to know darkness like this. But the darkest place I have ever been, the darkness of my childhood, no longer exists. We are lucky: the place we have known—the lake (though not as clear) and woods (though splotched with more houses)—still more or less exists. But the darkness I knew then has faded. The ever-larger small towns to the northwest and south have made sure of that. There simply is more light on the horizon and overhead. And so, the night sky I knew as a child is gone, because the darkness that held that sky is gone.

The term "shifting environmental baseline" describes how each new generation marks as reality the world as they experience it and the reality against which they will judge any change. But if that reality has been steadily diminished through the years, each new generation knows a living world less abundant and diverse than did those who came before. It's the idea that my two-year-old will never know the darkness I knew in these woods four decades ago, but when we walk down that same gravel road in summers to come, she will think it very dark, maybe the darkest place she has ever been.

And it is still dark at our lake cabin, just not as dark as it used to be. In that sense, it is the same as most anywhere people live. The places that are still primitively dark, such as the oceans, the Outback, the Amazon, are places

Hollywood Bowl Overlook, Los Angeles, California

most of us will never even visit—let alone inhabit. Their level of darkness is no longer our experience of night. In the urban areas where increasing numbers of us live—by 2050 some two-thirds of the world's human population—there is more and more artificial light, less and less natural darkness.

A good illustration of this new reality is that for most people living in cities around the world, our eyes seldom adjust from daylight to dark. Normally, as the world darkens, our eyes would shift to scotopic or "night-vision," moving from favoring "cones," which show us the world in color, to favoring "rods," which detect fainter light but not color. In natural conditions this happens over time—thirty minutes is good, a couple hours better. But in a modern city flooded with artificial light, this rarely happens at all. This is why a gas lamp in a modern city seems ridiculously dim. But to a nineteenth-century city dweller, eyes adjusted to darkness, these lamps would have seemed impressively bright.

We live our nights swamped in a darkness diluted with artificial light. As a result, we mostly have no idea what we are missing, what we are losing. We have no idea what it's like to be out in a naturally dark night.

<hr />

About twenty years ago, an amateur astronomer named John Bortle decided to make this clear. He had grown used to other astronomers—younger ones, especially—urging him to visit some stargazing spot they described as "so dark!" only to find there what he had found everywhere, that this new location was not nearly as dark as his companions believed. In 2001, he published the Bortle Dark-Sky Scale, which named nine "classes" of darkness. The scale begins at 9 (our brightest places—any of the world's cities, with rare exceptions) and progresses down to 1 (our darkest places, with no evidence of artificial light).

Ever since learning of Bortle's scale, I have been fascinated by the concept. But when I asked a National Park Service friend where I could experience "Bortle Class 1," he laughed and suggested Australia. What about here in the United States? Depending on whom you asked, he said, there were few if any places left in the lower forty-eight with that kind of darkness. When later I spent a night in Death Valley National Park with another Park Service friend, he told me that he had ranked the level of darkness in more than two hundred NPS locations and named only three as Bortle Class 1. Two of these he told me—"The Racetrack" in Death Valley and a spot along the Green River in southern Utah—and the third he kept a secret.

Think of this. Bortle Class 1 is natural darkness, night without artificial light—none on the horizon, none in the sky. It is night's darkness as it would have been for all of time before gas and then, especially, electric lighting. Which, for many rural places in the United States means until just a few decades ago. We have taken the natural state of things and—over the entire country—diminished it. We have introduced the artificial into the natural, and our experience of night is not what it was. We no longer experience the darkness that our ancestors— even, for many, our own grandparents—experienced.

Consider this too: on that scale of darkness, where 9 represents our lit-up cities and 1 this natural darkness, most Americans and Europeans and city dwellers worldwide live in Class 5 and above. That is, we rarely or never experience a night any darker than midway on the scale. So, our nights are not just a bit brighter than the nights of those who came before us knew, but a lot brighter.

Perhaps this makes sense in a city where we live immersed in artificial

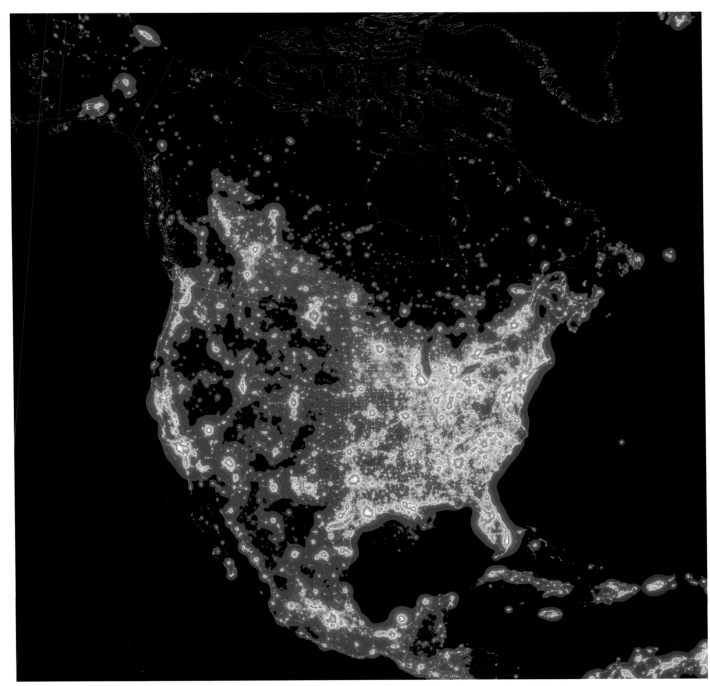

Map of North America's artificial sky brightness, from "The New World Atlas of Artificial Night Sky Brightness."
Courtesy of Fabio Falchi.

World map of artificial sky brightness, from "The New World Atlas of Artificial Night Sky Brightness." Courtesy of Fabio Falchi.

fear

It must be poor life that achieves freedom from fear.

—Aldo Leopold, *A Sand County Almanac*

The year after graduating from college I drove thirteen hundred miles from Minneapolis to Moab in a small white Subaru with no cruise control. After pressing the accelerator for eighteen hours, I reached the southern Utah desert long after midnight and pulled into a campground by the Colorado River. Shimmering stars stretched overhead, but the horizon around me loomed solidly black—no stars, no streetlights, nothing. My mind couldn't make sense of it, but I was too tired to care. At first light, I found I had reached a world where red-rock walls come down to the river in the morning and stars rise from cliff edge at night. I had traveled west to mountain bike the area's slickrock and to see some of my country's best starry skies. And I had come alone, hoping to overcome my fear of the dark.

After a few days among the relative crowds around Moab, I drove south to the Needles section of Canyonlands National Park. No open sites remained in the campground, but if I wanted, I could grab a permit and camp in the back-country. I felt a quick wave of nerves but figured that yes, this was exactly why I was here. I drove a few miles before parking, stomped out into the wilderness, set up my tent, and waited for night to arrive. I was young and thought I was

Landscape Arch, Arches National Park, Utah

Bryce Canyon National Park, Utah

day's ceiling rolls back to reveal night's vault of stars. I want her to feel the natural fear that arises as our usual experience of life fades away. I want her to be smart when she's out at night, but I don't want her to be afraid of "the dark."

Outside at night there is a good fear, a knowing you don't have control, a respect for what you can't see—as well as for what you can. Your focus draws upward. And inward, if you allow it—to your thoughts, memories, and emotions. A fear that's more like exhilaration? That's part of a starry night.

Black Rock Desert, Nevada

knowledge

What did the scientists know about what I had done?
How could they explain what had happened to me and
the strange sensations I had known?

–Sigurd Olson, "Northern Lights"

had always loved the night sky—growing up spending weeks at the lake every summer ensured I would—but I knew next to nothing about it. When it came to constellations, I knew Orion because of the iconic three-star "belt," and I knew the "Big Dipper." But that almost didn't count, I was soon to learn, because it wasn't actually a constellation but rather an "asterism," a grouping of stars without that official designation. Recently into my thirties, living in a city surrounded by some of the darkest geography left in the United States, I decided to finally learn the stars.

Back then that did not involve staring at a computer screen. Instead, I began to pull books from local shelves. More than once, I spent a Friday evening sitting on a bookstore floor with astronomy books spread around me. Phones that show what you should see when you hold them toward the sky? Those did not exist. Instead, there were star maps on the printed page. This time reminds me of the moments I first met lifelong friends. The friend you talked with last weekend and have known for twenty-five years—there was a time when the two of you had never met. Or, your partner? A few marry their kindergarten pal, but most of us live decades without knowing the person with whom we will share our life.

For me, it was like this with a handful of constellations. (And I mean here the classical Greek sky, knowing that Indigenous cultures around the world have long had their own constellations too.) I especially liked Scorpius and Sagittarius, which for North American viewers lie close to summer's southwestern horizon. Scorpius, the Scorpion with the red star Antares as its eye, and Sagittarius, the Archer with the Milky Way steaming from its "teapot" spout. These were easily recognizable shapes, but for me they meant something more. The fact they were low on the horizon when I went out before bed made them feel closer. They became the constellations that linked my two homes. I could see them while standing behind my Albuquerque house and imagine being back on the dock at the lake, where the two constellations rose just above the black silhouettes of shoreline pines. These were graduate school years when I was driving from New Mexico to Minnesota for summers and for winter breaks. A good twenty-four hours of driving between the city where I worked and studied and the lake where I went to see my family and write. Looking for love, living on next to nothing—whenever I see those two constellations, I think of that time, and I probably always will.

One constellation I had never seen, though I must have looked at it count-less times, was Cygnus, the Swan. The shape of Cygnus, with its wings, neck, and tail feathers outlined by stars, is one of those relatively few constellations that immediately make sense. Ever since I recognized it, I've liked the thought that this beautiful bird will be flying above me at night forever. In summer, Cygnus flies straight overhead at the lake, and its main star, Deneb, combined with Vega (in the constellation Lyra, the Lyre) and Altair (in the constellation

Fort Churchill State Historic Park, Nevada

Aquila, the Eagle) make up what we know as the Summer Triangle. Like the Big Dipper, the Summer Triangle is an asterism rather than a constellation, and a shape that once recognized is easily found again.

Knowing some constellations began to connect me with the night sky. I was no longer looking up at an indecipherable mess of stars. I could see some patterns, and that drew me closer. But I never really learned the constellations in the way I had imagined I would. I'd had visions of being the guy who—when called on by a gathered group or by a date-who-was-ready-to-be-impressed—could unlock the mysteries of the nighttime sky. Aside from these few familiar shapes, I never achieved that goal.

Instead, what I learned almost immediately about the constellations is that when I went outside, I could not see them. For one thing, no matter how creatively my astronomy books showed me the shapes, when I got out under the stars, I just could not see such constellations as Monoceros, the Unicorn, or Ophiuchus, the Serpent Bearer. It may simply be that our modern lack of engagement with such creatures or livelihoods makes it difficult to envision them in the sky. While some of the Southern Hemisphere constellations named in the nineteenth century might seem amusing to us now—Microscopium (the Microscope), Circinus (the Compass)—more familiar shapes would likely be easier to find. But the biggest reason I could not see the constellations twenty years ago is the same reason so many of us can't see them today: light pollution.

———

In a way, learning about light pollution was like learning the constellations in that both were something I had looked at all my life but had never really seen. Though "all my life" is not entirely true. When I was a child in the 1970s, the

Joshua Tree National Park, California

Fort Churchill State Historic Park, Nevada

Las Vegas, Nevada

light pollution in northern Minnesota was almost nonexistent. On the Bortle Dark-Sky Scale those skies would have been Class 2. When Fabio Falchi and his colleagues created their original "World Atlas of the Artificial Night Sky Brightness," they estimated back in time to show the US night sky in 1970 and 1950. The 1950 sky, a time when the country held only 100 million people, is long gone. It is the sky of grandparents and great-grandparents growing up on farms. So often in my presentations I hear stories from this generation about the sky they knew as children. I won't forget one elderly woman telling me how she would take her horse into the night meadow and, while it grazed, lie on its back to watch the Milky Way spill overhead.

While researching *The End of Night*, the estimate I found most troubling is that eight out of ten children born in the United States today will never live where they can see the Milky Way. On Falchi's Atlas the sky from 1970—the first sky I would have seen, the area where our lake lies—is black. As a child I would have known a sky that few children know in the United States now.

And that's because of light pollution.

Light pollution is something that once you see it, you see it everywhere. There's an old saying that no one knows who discovered water but that it probably wasn't a fish. Something similar could be said of light pollution. Most of us live so immersed in the sea of artificial light created by our cities and suburbs that we can't imagine night being any different. In fact, almost anyone younger than about forty who has grown up in Western countries or in cities around the world has probably never known a night without light pollution.

And so, I had set out to learn the constellations and instead learned why I could not see them. I learned terms such as *skyglow* (the diffuse spread of light over any city) and *light trespass* (light shining from one property onto another)

Shiprock, New Mexico

and *glare* (blinding light). And I learned to see these types of light pollution all over the place. I had long remembered with fondness those winter nights in my boyhood Minneapolis when after a big snowfall the sky would be a push-pop orange and the whole night illuminated. You could play outside and see clearly in the weirdly bright night. It felt adventurous to pull on boots and coat and mittens and head out into the unplowed city's glow. But now I realized that warm glow had been caused by light pollution—the pink-orange light from high-pressure sodium streetlights reflecting off the clouds and snow. I suddenly saw how many billboards featured lights shining either straight into the sky or bouncing off their intended target and from there into the sky. And I realized how much glaring light shone straight into our eyes, our bedrooms, our backyards.

This knowledge didn't add to my experience of a starry night, except maybe for this: it helped me to realize what I was missing. The sky I saw over Albuquerque was nothing like the starry night I could be seeing. It's remarkable to think that few of us anymore really know what the sky overhead looks like—or would look like if not for all our lights.

A stunning image from 2003 shows the usual nighttime sky over the photographer's suburban home side by side with the sky as it looked one night when a power outage darkened eastern North America. In the how-it-always-looks view, a cloud of skyglow blocks every star. In the power-outage-for-a-night view, the Milky Way hangs behind the house like a glittering curtain. Whenever I see this image, I remember Emerson's words from the early nineteenth century about how people would react "if the stars came one night in a thousand years." It's revealing that in Emerson's age, the stars were so numerous, so *everyday,* so—probably to teenagers of the era—boring, that he used them to make his point about humanity taking nature for granted. In the twenty-first century, most of us have never seen a sky that would have been common in his time. That experience—the heavens made visible—would simply have been part of daily life.

But knowing what I am missing has made me grateful for those times I do see an unpolluted sky. I know what I'm seeing is rare, that not many people in the modern world share such a sight. And with the ever-growing number of people in cities, so many will never know it. And by "know" I mean experience firsthand. Because we can "know" the night sky by looking at a computer screen, by staring at our phones, even by looking at books. But that way of knowing has limits.

In his essay "Northern Lights," published in 1956, Sigurd Olson reflected on the knowledge that comes from firsthand experience. A popular writer during his lifetime, Olson penned straightforward essays about his experiences in the Boundary Waters between Minnesota and Ontario. In "Northern Lights," Olson told the story of ice skating on a clear lake at night. He wrote this at a time when Americans were increasingly seeing scientific advancements in medicine, space exploration, consumer goods, and on. Olson acknowledged that the northern lights can be understood through scientific explanation. But, he explained, this isn't the only way to know these lights. Myth and story and poetry are ways to know them as well. And no textbook could explain the northern lights better than could an experience of skating with them on a frozen northern lake.

We now have more scientific knowledge of the night sky than ever before. I have always felt this kind of knowledge adds to my experience of the world. Because these facts and figures are so often utterly amazing, often unfathomable, knowing them adds to my awe. We can bring this knowledge with us when we step outside. But go outside we must, if we really want to know a starry night.

White Sands National Park, New Mexico

While my daughter doesn't "know" light pollution, artificial lights already shape her experience of the night. I am grateful I know what a natural starry night looks like, for I will want to bring her there as soon as I can. I want her to know the constellations, to know the numbers and facts, to see the deep-space photographs on her computer screen. But the knowledge I want most for her comes from standing under a truly dark sky, as her ancestors have all through time.

Bonsai Rock, Lake Tahoe, Nevada

solace

*But in prison, where I was hardly even a number, the stars
made me feel differently. They helped me to understand that
I was part of a greater thing, not the greater thing itself.*

—Ken Lamberton, "Night Time"

I was being interviewed on the radio, talking about the value of a starry night. A man called to say that when he was a teenager, there had been a lot of fighting and yelling at home, and being in the house he felt trapped. So, he would hop into his pickup and drive out to the countryside, climb onto the hood, and watch the night sky. He said being alone under the sky helped put things into perspective, gave him a chance to escape the hard times back home, made him feel there were other possibilities in the world.

When I think of this story, I think of the word "solace." That sense of comfort and consolation in times of distress. Surely, people have found solace in a starry night since the beginning of time. As hard as things might be on Earth, you could look up and feel some other reality existed. Maybe it's the timelessness of stars, how they have always been there. Maybe it's knowing they are so far away, and so many, and how that can make our problems feel smaller. It's having the perspective to see beyond our immediate concerns. It's what Charlie Chaplin once said: "Life is a tragedy when seen close-up, but a comedy in long-shot."

In his essay "Night Time," Ken Lamberton writes about being in prison and how most nights he couldn't see the stars. Either he was locked inside, or glare filled the prison yard. But every so often—maybe during a power outage or while being moved from one location to another—he would glimpse a starry sky. He describes the freedom he felt seeing the stars he had loved before prison, the sky he couldn't wait to see once he was released. He tells how stunned he was that most people choose to lock themselves inside away from the stars, while he who desperately wanted to see them could not.

For prisoners, slaves, soldiers, victims of violence, even someone simply lovesick or heartbroken—the night sky has always been a source of solace. For all of us, and for free.

But now, with our overuse and misuse of artificial light at night, we have taken this comfort from most Americans, from most Europeans, from city dwellers around the world. What solace can we take from a sky that offers only a hazy gray-dark canvas with maybe a few drips of light? No longer spectacular, no longer awe-inspiring. No longer something you would want to lie back with your family to watch. No longer something to spark contemplation, reflection, perspective. No longer a source of solace at a time when we could really use some.

When I think of the world my daughter will know, I often feel distress. She will never know the natural world that I have known, because much of that world no longer exists. In the five decades since I was born, for example, the world has lost some two-thirds of its wildlife. In that same time period, three billion birds have disappeared from North America alone. In sub-Saharan Africa the

Coronado Island, San Diego, California

Rocky Mountain National Park, Colorado

solitude

Then I had a dog, and this changed my relation to night.

I won't forget bringing her home, the car winding its way down into Santa Fe from the Los Alamos house where she had been born. It was November, and we drove in the dark with snowflakes floating to earth around us. On the passenger seat my puppy lay curled in the blue plastic laundry basket I had brought along to keep her contained on the ninety-minute drive. When I stopped in Santa Fe to dash into a grocery store for some dinner, I left the motor running with the hope she wouldn't wake. This was the first night in a fifteen-year relationship that would shape my life.

I was living in Albuquerque, working as a waiter and going to graduate school. I had read that a dog's basic needs are "attention and exercise," and luckily for her I had plenty of time for both. First thing every morning we took a long walk together and then most evenings another. And all her life, almost every night, the last thing we did before bed was to go for one more.

Santa Fe, New Mexico

I was living near Old Town, the plaza where in 1706 the city took root surrounded by single- and two-story adobe buildings. The modern downtown eventually rose a mile away, and Old Town was now mostly for tourists and the stores that catered to them. At night, the place was deserted, and in the hour before midnight we seldom saw another soul. I would hop on my mountain bike and Luna would race alongside. We would cross over Rio Grande Boulevard and cut into Old Town, where she would blast into alleys and leap over low adobe courtyard walls. A little chapel tucked behind an art gallery was left unlocked, a sanctuary where people lit votives and left personal messages in crayon and pen to particular saints. So much history had passed here—the narrow one-way streets and walkways were filled with friendly ghosts, quiet, and relative dark. All day long, I would look forward to Old Town with Luna at night.

Just east of the plaza lay a small neighborhood park without lights. I would sometimes steer us there and stop to watch Orion rise above where the city's butterscotch streetlights ended at the base of the Sandia Mountains, the winter sky growing more familiar each time.

I began to understand how unusual it was to be out enjoying the night, especially alone. Simply put, it seemed no one else was around. I don't mean out on the town, enjoying food and drink. I mean outside enjoying the darkness, the stars, the sounds and scents of the natural night. Roasting green chiles infused the autumn air, as did in most months smoke from fires fueled with piñon pine. I began to treasure the sensation of how the world felt slowed in speed and reduced in size, how I could breathe and relax. I came to savor the solitude of being out alone at night.

At the lake in Minnesota, I mostly watched the sky alone as well, standing on the dock or paddling the canoe. And in the years that would follow my time in Albuquerque—especially when I was working on *The End of Night*—I often found myself alone in the darkness. It was true in Maine when I drove up Cadillac Mountain to watch the sun set and the night arrive and had the distinct impression that everyone else was driving down off the mountain. It was true on the Grand Canyon's North Rim when I lay on the ancient rocks and felt as though floating amid a sea of stars. It was true in southern Utah's Natural Bridges National Monument, the parking areas empty, the trails deserted, the Bortle Class 2 skies all mine.

In Old Town, at the lake, in these other places and since, I felt a heightened alertness and attention to my surroundings—that feeling of being wonderfully in the moment, the intimacy of only being where I am.

Some of this is circumstance—I haven't had a lifetime of being told I should be frightened at night, as have some of my friends. I have never had to endure unwanted advances, or deal with an ever-present potential of being attacked. I have lived where there has been little threat of real danger—a luxury that too many people around the world don't share. But still, the good solitude of which I am speaking can be found in different ways. A friend in Mexico City who keeps his child from the neighborhood park for fear of violence lets her instead climb onto their building's roof at night to see the stars.

Sometimes the solitude of a starry night is literal, but other times it comes in the company of a friend, a group of strangers at a star party, at the edges of a presentation in a national park. Either way, a starry night offers an opportunity to know, too, the solitude of every human life.

We all are alone, on some level—no one can inhabit our body, no one can live our life, no one can die our death. With its numbers and distances that bend our brain, a starry night raises questions like "Who am I?" "What will

Outhouse, Bodie State Historic Park, Wyoming

Casino Borealis, Reno, Nevada

my life be?" "Have I lived my time wisely?" and offers the chance to answer such questions for ourself rather than have them answered for us.

In this way, under the stars in our solitude, we join with everyone else.

When I finished my degree in Albuquerque, I moved to Nevada and bought a small white house with sky blue trim in Reno's Old Southwest neighborhood. Luna and I shared a wonderful four years there, in part because it's so easy to get out of the city. A seven-minute drive brought us to the foothills for an hour-long hike. But we kept our habit of walking our neighborhood before bed, too. We would walk four blocks to a local park, past the pale blue glow of televisions behind window curtains. Once, on a snowy night, we walked past a man in his garage cleaning shot quail, and he gave Luna a wing that she proudly carried away, her pawprints warm blooms in the sidewalk snow.

But usually, just as in Old Town, if we waited late enough, we walked alone. We would travel those blocks seeing no one, and we would have the park to ourselves. Being out at night like that, even under a sky missing most of its stars, the solitude was like a secret I'd been told, one I savored and held close.

The solitude of night feels like a gift. A chance to not feel so surrounded by people with their cars and trucks and buildings, their speed and noise and light. During the day, I am too often part of all that. How can we not be? But at night, if we are lucky, we can still know the possibilities solitude brings.

Eastern Sierra moonrise, Lone Pine, California

moonlight

Suppose you attend to the suggestions which the moon makes for one
month.... What if one moon has come and gone, with its world of poetry,
its weird teachings, its oracular suggestions,—so divine a creature freighted
with hints for me, and I have not used her,—one moon gone by unnoticed?

—Henry David Thoreau, "Night and Moonlight"

love being surprised by the moon. I'll be driving at dusk and suddenly it will appear above the horizon, glowing and huge, as though lit from within, set afloat, and lifted by flames. Other times, after what seems like weeks, I'll catch sight of its wisp of curved light in the low western sky. But while I have always loved the moon, when I read Thoreau's essay from 1850, I realized that I had never really "attended" to it. I took as a challenge his words, "Suppose you attend to the suggestions which the moon makes for one month?" and decided that for thirty nights—from "new" to last waning crescent—I would be out beneath the moon.

I decided this during summer, a time when night's warmth would make my quest more likely to succeed. And I would do it at the lake. Our cabin faces west, so my horizon across the water is a shoreline of pines with the night sky just above. I can sit at the end of the redwood dock, bare feet in cool water, and wait for the Milky Way to emerge.

And here is where I found the first moon. Just above the trees, a barely visible crescent that if you weren't watching would likely drop from view before you noticed.

Those first few moons were easy—I could savor the twilight, the crescent taking shape, moving toward first quarter. And all this in the hours just after sunset, a perfect time to see the sky. As the month progressed, the moon turned larger, building toward half a moon high overhead, until came the nights around full when it rose opposite the setting sun, climbing from the woods behind our house to cast the sun's reflected light across the lake's ripples and waves. Gradually, the moon's rise came later and later, so that finally I was setting an alarm for the wee small hours and pulling myself out of bed and into the night. It then disappeared for a few days before once again showing above the far shore, that faint curve of light. It's a pattern that, having made it familiar, will always be part of my life.

I was living with Luna in Reno then, in our small house where it felt like the largest room was the never-ending foothills on the edge of town. We couldn't have known before we moved to Reno how accessible and wonderful that open space would be. We had left a good life in New Mexico, where Luna had lived her first four years and I had lived eight. But graduate school called, and when I drove the moving truck west out of the Rio Grande Valley, she hopped up onto her blue dog bed on the passenger seat, my copilot. The next four years would be a kind of "dog heaven" for her. Every morning and every evening we would drive to a trailhead, and I would set her free to run while I walked, lost in thought, savoring our repeated paths.

First snow, Reno, Nevada

Emerald Bay, Lake Tahoe, California

What makes for a good life? For me, it has been regular patterns—walking with my dog, cooking and eating good food, hot baths at night, crawling into a comfortable bed. Occasional surprise and excitement, yes, but these regular daily patterns have given me the deepest pleasure. When Thoreau describes the moon as "so divine a creature freighted with hints for me," I think of this. Once you become acquainted with the moon, you know where in the sky to find it, you know when it will be back. Every month, I anticipate the rise of a nearly full, full, and just past full moon, and in this return feel again the pleasure of a pattern repeated. No matter what is going on in my life or the life of the world, I know the moon will be there sharing its light.

~

Part of the moon's magic is the way it takes us to places remembered or imagined, the way it links us to who we were and to those who came before. Watching the moon and stars, we do what humans have always done, we see what humans have always seen. Because of light pollution, we see less today than what those before us saw, but the thread remains. This connection to the past, this sense of being allowed back to a place and time where some ancient world goes on— nothing brings this feeling more than seeing the moon.

For me the moon often seems to show at important intervals, to mark experiences in my life. If the moon were always in the sky, this feeling wouldn't be the same. I know I won't forget these nights: the moon above a walking bridge in Venice when I was eighteen and away from my family for the first time; it shining above Gail's house the summer she said no; the night another love said yes as we stood on a stone arch by a city lake; the first time I took my daughter out to introduce her to the sky.

Joshua Tree National Park, California

Black Rock Desert, Nevada

Golden Gate Bridge, Marin County, California

wildness

t was late August at the cabin, the time of year when the days still feel like summer, but the nights feel as though autumn is gathering in the woods across the lake. That hint of a chill, that crispness in the air, the wood smoke from someone's fire.

I walked out onto the dock. A yellow moon burned low in the southern sky, its light rippling off water brushed by a slight breeze. Just a few lights around the shore, maybe a fishing boat in the distance, a solitary fish jump splash, a woman's echoing laugh.

Suddenly, a long howl rose from the woods beneath the moon. I first thought "coyote?" and then understood, *wolf.* What stuns me still is the way this ancient wild sound, ringing out on a summer night in a northern forest, reverberated through my body. The wolf was deep in the woods and I was a short dash from my door, yet this primal sensation coursed through me. I listened for a few seconds, then hurried inside.

We have wolves in the woods around the cabin, but they keep their secrets. I think of them as drifting among the pines and oaks and evaporating like smoke when they know we are near. Every once in a while there's a story—a wolf hit by a motorcycle, a wolf seen crossing a lane in the evening. But in four decades of coming to the lake I have heard a howl only twice. This time I knew I was in no danger—and still, I felt the instinctual fear that has been passed down, the feeling of not being king of the world. When I think of that feeling now, I want it again. I wish I could go back to that moment, turn toward the gravel lane, and set off toward that sound.

~

At night, the wild world comes alive. So many creatures have evolved over millions of years to be nocturnal, meaning they need night's natural darkness in order to survive. Many more species are crepuscular, meaning they are most active at dawn and dusk. From the tiniest insect to the largest mammal, species have evolved to use night's darkness as time to move and feed, migrate and mate. And on a planet increasingly crowded with humans, night has become even more important to the wild world. Scientists have found that to avoid people and to use what space remains, more species are shifting their activities into the dark. One study in Nepal found the same jungle paths used by people during the day were the paths used by tigers at night.

One example of night's wildness is that of migrating birds. In North America alone some four hundred species migrate after dark. During spring and fall migrations, ornithologists use weather surveillance radar to track the great flocks moving north and south along the continent's flyways. Many of these night migrations are made of songbirds, and it's sometimes possible to stand outside and hear them passing over, their chips and chirps as they keep tabs on

Wind River Range, Wyoming

Lassen Volcanic National Park, California

each other. Whenever I have a chance to hear this—to witness these migrations more with my ears than my eyes—I feel welcomed into a hidden world. Here is ancient life going on around us that normally we don't notice. Out at night to watch the stars, wildness passes overhead.

The importance of night's darkness for the wild world makes the problem of light pollution all the more serious. We are just beginning to understand the negative impacts on this natural life from too much artificial light. Life on Earth evolved with bright days and dark nights, and this life needs both natural light and natural darkness. Knowing this, it's easy to imagine the negative impact from our use of electric and electronic light, whether scientific studies reflect this yet or not. As one biologist told me, "Imagine how dimming the sun would impact the world's life, and this is exactly what we are doing by increasing our light at night. We could expect the effects to be just as pronounced."

The effect on insects is a prime example. Many of us have learned the importance of bees, butterflies, and other pollinating insects. But pollinators are active at night too, especially moths. Many people have noticed they don't see as many insects as they used to. We no longer notice a "moth snowstorm" around a streetlight on a summer's night, or the splatter across our car's windshield on a late-night drive. Researchers have confirmed these observations with studies that show an alarming drop in insect populations. Their once great numbers no longer enliven our wild natural night. Habitat destruction, climate change, and pesticide use are the main causes, but light pollution contributes as well.

What's maddening is that light pollution is so unnecessary. Indeed, a basic definition—the overuse and misuse of artificial light at night—reflects this fact. With insects and other wildlife already facing so many enormous challenges, it's frustrating that artificial light at night would be an additional burden.

Mohave County, Arizona

Wee Thump Joshua Tree Wilderness, Nevada

mystery

In my first memory of this life I am five years old and standing on the dock with my father watching satellites pass through sugary spreads of stars. It is summertime at the lake in northern Minnesota, to where I have returned every summer since. Why is that memory my first? Why not something else from my five years on the planet? Maybe that's just where the film starts, where I had reached an age to begin putting down memories that four decades later I still can recall. But maybe it says something about the power of the moment, that of everything I had experienced so far, this one made its mark.

Now I have a two-year-old daughter who has learned to point out the moon, and who sometimes says "no stars" when presented with a city sky. I have no idea whether she will remember the moments she has lived so far, but we are conscious of the experiences we give her. For example, we share her with our parents as much as possible, hoping the time she spends with her grand-parents will shape her life long after they are gone.

Joshua Tree National Park, California

My mother and father are both in their eighties. The man on the dock in my first memory is twenty years younger than I am now, and the days—and nights—keep coming. I cannot imagine the world without my parents. I don't want to. Yet if life takes its natural course, someday they will be gone, and I will still be here.

I sometimes think of the first full moon that will come after they pass, the first moon in my life to shine down without finding them here. I know the same will happen for me, that one night a full moon will rise, and I will be nowhere to see it. But these thoughts are too big. How can we no longer exist? How can anything exist in the first place? Especially when everything we know tells us an endless black universe surrounds our blue-green home, how came this world to be?

⸺

We are a species that adores the light and fears the dark, and mystery is a kind of darkness. We aren't good at letting it be. We aren't good at engaging. We avoid, ignore, or shoo it away. We try to explain, we try to control.

And the unknown is frightening—I know this firsthand. All my adult life I have sometimes feared the way my body has felt. A stomachache, a headache, a lump in my throat. They say it is "only" anxiety, but the sensations are real, and sometimes I have endured a panic that stays for days, or weeks, or worse. But each time I make it through my fear, the world opens in a new way. If I once took something for granted, I no longer do. Whatever I loved before this mysterious fear, I love even more.

When we lose the night sky, we lose a chance to become familiar with mystery. As much as we know about the stars, so much has yet to be known.

Logan Pass, Glacier National Park, Montana

Fort Churchill State Historic Park, Nevada

And even when we have studied something so long—like the moon—that we have packed up our instruments and moved on, mystery remains. Why are so many of us pulled by the moon to look up in wonder? (And why some seem immune to that pull is mystery of another kind.) Walking out at night and seeing a starry sky, coming face to face with the universe, presents us with something greater than we can grasp. All the stars we ever see are shining within our own galaxy—the Milky Way Galaxy—and beyond our galaxy are countless others. We cannot fathom what we are seeing, let alone what we are not. Where did we come from? Where do we go? What is all this we are looking at? By preserving the night sky, we preserve this experience.

What if a starry night were part of every human life? How might it change the way we live? What if the experience of a starry night were a common way of learning about all that we cannot control? What if it were something every parent shared with every child, a way of explaining when there are no words? Sharing a starry night with a child is like giving them another language, one that speaks intangibles. Why not teach our children that mystery is a fact of life?

I like the thought that my father showed me the stars that night for this reason. Knowing him, he probably just wanted to look for shooting stars. But even if we don't think about it consciously, we tend to want to share the stars with those we love. It's a way to communicate a respect for beauty and mystery, a respect for the brief time we get to be alive.

In Luna's last summer, when she had lost much of what had made her the greatest dog I have ever known, and the vet told me she had only weeks left, I decided to say goodbye at the cabin in Minnesota. On her last night, we went out onto the dock under a waning gibbous, one of those big moons that rises late and stays through the night. I sat on the dock with my legs crossed and brought Luna onto my lap—the same way she had crawled onto my lap as a puppy fifteen years before. In some cultures, I would have hummed or sang a song of the dying, a song of goodbye. Too much of my own culture, I sat quietly, holding my friend, my face alternately in her fur and turned toward the sky.

There was nothing I could do to keep her with me, nothing I could do to take us back to days spent hiking at dusk on the desert city's edge, the owlets tucked into the cliffside, their mother curving toward us in silent flight, the day's light draining and the first stars taking their positions in the twilit sky. The life she knew is the best thing I have so far done with mine. But I could do nothing to keep the end from coming.

She has been gone now six years, and I like that if I were able to go back, I would do nothing differently. I would give her the same life, and I would be out on the same dock where, so many years before, my father pointed me toward the Milky Way and wordlessly said, *Beauty and mystery and life, here you go.* I would hold my friend and say thank you, again and again.

———

Two loving parents, four grandparents alive well into my twenties, a family cabin on a northern lake where I first learned about night—I am lucky to have grown up in the circumstances I did. So many people live where they can barely see a dozen stars, where the moon can rise and cross the sky unnoticed, where they have no choice about the night they know. But for those who do, we can choose to have the light we need but not more than we need. We can choose

Lake Tahoe, Nevada

Supermoonrise, Mohave County, Arizona

I learned as much as I could about perfecting the technique while enjoying the capabilities of new digital cameras able to use high ISO in ways previously not possible. I would lead a field trip every semester to Nevada's Fort Churchill State Historic Park for night photography, and the students loved it. Many would tell me that it was the best field trip of their entire academic career. My photos ended up catching the attention of an outdoor tourism website, and then Dr. Scott Slovic put me in touch with Paul Bogard to work together on this project.

Most of my nighttime images at the time were taken in Nevada, but Paul and I decided to spread the coverage across the West. I went out several times during the summers of 2017 and 2018 and spent the entire summer of 2019 collecting nighttime images. After more than a decade of shooting at night, my main advice is to use a sturdy tripod, a fast wide-angle lens, and a camera that does well at high-sensitivity settings (ISO). Good planning and patience are two other helpful skills. For Milky Way photos, astronomy apps for smartphones are invaluable. Always remember that the galactic core of the Milky Way is next to the constellation of Scorpius, and the five nights before and after a new moon are typically the best.

My favorite image is the one of Washington's Mount Rainier, for which I had planned over a year in advance and reserved a backcountry campsite near the Sunrise Visitor Center on the west side of the park. In 2014, I accidentally found a great location for night photography there and decided to return when I had more experience and better camera gear. It was a cloudy day during the drive to the mountain, and the situation did not look promising. I arrived in the late afternoon and walked about four miles to my campsite. An hour before dark, I walked another mile to the viewpoint and was disappointed to see that the entire mountain was hidden in the clouds. I almost gave up and returned to camp, but then a hiker passed me. When I told him about my disappointing situation, he quickly said, "Man, all you need to do is walk another couple miles up this trail. You'll end up above the clouds, and the view is amazing." I am so glad that I followed his advice. For several hours, I sat on a rock and enjoyed the most incredible view: Mount Rainier surrounded by stars with the clouds below the peak like a bowl of cotton candy.

Glacier National Park, Montana

ACKNOWLEDGMENTS

We thank Dr. Scott Slovic, who first brought us together on this project. For both of us, Scott has been a source of unfailing support over the years. Without his interest in our work, this book would not exist.

Thank you to Scott for his opening words, and to Karen Trevino for hers.

We thank all the good people at the University of Nevada Press. We are thrilled to have this book be published by a press we both admire. To Margaret Dalrymple, JoAnne Banducci, Sara Vélez Mallea, Sara Hendricksen, Iris Saltus, and Jinni Fontana—we are grateful for your support of this book.

Our thanks as well to Justin Race for his initial excitement about the idea. Thanks to Clark Whitehorn, who immediately expressed his support and helped the project move forward. And, especially, we thank Alrica Goldstein for her enthusiasm about the book and her guiding hand in bringing it into the world.

PB: My thanks first to Beau Rogers, whose photographs fill this book. It's humbling and exciting to have such stunning images placed alongside my prose.

Thanks to all those who work to protect darkness around the world. Thanks especially to the folks at the International Dark-Sky Association, including Ruskin Hartley and John Barentine. Thank you as well to Fabio Falchi for his Atlas, and for his tireless work against light pollution in northern Italy.

Several of the chapter epigraphs come from essays I collected for *Let There*

Be Night: Testimony on Behalf of the Dark. To Ken Lamberton, Janisse Ray, Robin Wall Kimmerer, and Kathleen Dean Moore, my gratitude again for your words.

My thanks to new colleagues at Hamline University and to past colleagues at James Madison University, Wake Forest University, and Northland College. I am grateful for your friendship and support.

Love to Rose and Ron Hilk. To my parents, John and Judith Bogard. To Caroline, and to The Bub.